One Happy Classroom

by Charnan Simon

illustrated by Rebecca McKillip Thornburgh

Children's Press®
A Division of Scholastic Inc.
New York • Toronto • London • Auckland • Sydney
Mexico City • New Delhi • Hong Kong
Danbury, Connecticut

for Doris Kozlowski,
Adrianne Johnson, and
Georgie Vavra—and all the
other teachers of happy
classrooms in the world —C.S.

for David—R.McK.T.

Reading Consultant
Linda Cornwell
Learning Resource
Consultant
Indiana Department
of Education

Library of Congress Cataloging-in-Publication Data
Simon, Charnan.
One happy classroom / by Charnan Simon ; illustrated by Rebecca McKillip
Thornburgh.
  p. cm. — (A rookie reader)
Summary: Activities in a happy, busy kindergarten classroom introduce the
numbers one to ten.
ISBN 0-516-20318-5 (lib. bdg.)—ISBN 0-516-26154-1 (pbk.)
[1. Kindergarten—Fiction. 2. Schools—Fiction. 3. Counting.]
I. Thornburgh, Rebecca McKillip, ill. II. Title. III. Series.
PZ7.S6035On 1997
  [E] —dc20
                                    96-21172
                                       CIP
                                       AC

Printed in China
11 12 R 09 08   62

One happy classroom.

Two smiling teachers.

4

Three leaning towers

made by four busy builders.

Five show-and-tellers.

Six good listeners.

Seven great painters

using eight
different
colors.

Nine pairs of partners

LUNCHROOM →

15

Ten crunchy apples.

17

**Nine
high climbers
over eight
hide-and-seekers.**

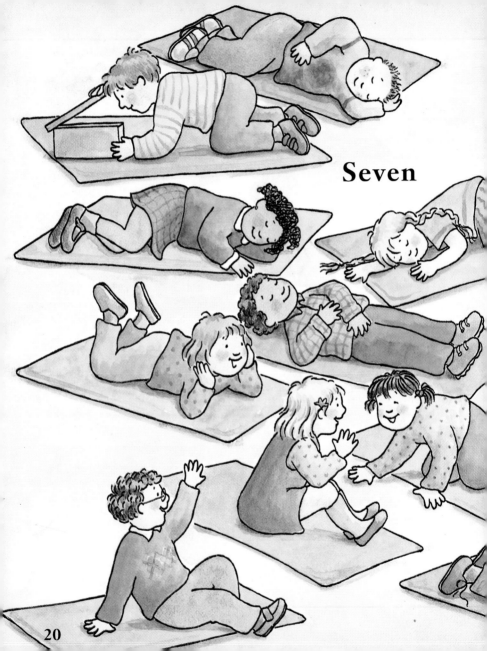

Seven

20

quiet

resters.

21

Six in a hurry!

Five big projects.

Four busy workers.

Three clean cages.

Two stuck zippers.

29

One happy classroom.

31

Word List (52 Words)

a	different	made	show
and	eight	nine	six
apples	five	of	smiling
big	four	one	stuck
builders	good	over	teachers
busy	great	painters	tellers
by	happy	pairs	ten
cages	hide	partners	three
classroom	high	projects	towers
clean	hurry	quiet	two
climbers	in	resters	using
colors	leaning	seekers	workers
crunchy	listeners	seven	zippers

About the Author

Charnan Simon lives in Madison, Wisconsin, with her husband, Tom Kazunas, and her two daughters, Ariel and Hana. She was an editor at *Cricket* magazine, and she sometimes works at a children's bookstore called Pooh Corner. Mostly, though, she enjoys spending time with her family and reading and writing books.

About the Illustrator

Rebecca McKillip Thornburgh grew up in Hollidaysburg, Pennsylvania, and studied fine art at Bryn Mawr College. To make the pictures for this book, she spent lots of time in the happy classrooms of her daughters, Blair and Alice. Rebecca lives with Blair, Alice, and her husband, David, in Philadelphia.